Original title:

Quasar Quips

Author: Alec Donovan

ISBN HARDBACK: 978-1-80567-847-2

ISBN PAPERBACK: 978-1-80567-968-4

Ethereal Euphoria

In the night sky they twinkle bright,
Distant stars with a wink and a light.
They gather for a cosmic chat,
Sharing jokes like a playful cat.

One claims to be a superstar,
While another chuckles, not too far.
With laughter bouncing off the moon,
They dance to an asteroid's tune.

A comet races, they all cheer loud,
Shooting jokes, making jokes proud.
Galaxies giggle with glee,
Orbiting humor, wild and free.

Planets join in with a spin and sway,
Making puns in a jovial way.
Celestial beings, they can't sit still,
In this vastness, they find the thrill.

Cosmic Chortles

In a galaxy not too far,
A star laughed at a rusty car.
'Why drift when you can glide?
Just take a ride on a comet's side!'

The black holes host a funny show,
While aliens dance to an old disco.
Their feet move fast, but don't ask why,
Now, space is where they learned to fly!

Planetary Puns

Why did Mars blush, you might ask?
Because it was caught in a big, bold task.
To woo Venus with a meteorite,
But her laughter was pure delight!

Jupiter tried to bake a pie,
But the oven's gravity made it fly.
The planets giggled in their dance,
As the pie did its cosmic prance!

Space-Time Shenanigans

Time travel's fun, but here's the catch,
You might end up with the wrong batch!
A dino in a space suit wears a crown,
Saying, 'Why are we in this weird town?'

The wormholes play hide and seek,
With trajectories that are quite unique.
One minute you're here, the next on Mars,
Looking for quirky interstellar bars!

Orbiting Humor

The moon cracked jokes on the milky way,
While Earth's folks laughed all day.
'This orbit's great, but what's the rush?
Let's toast to comets, and make a hush!'

Neptune wore a hat with stars,
Claiming, 'I'm the king of all bizarre!'
His subjects chuckled with glee,
'In this vast cosmos, we're all silly!'

Gravity of Gags

Why did the star refuse to shine?
It couldn't see a reason, so it crossed the line!
Did you hear about the black hole's plan?
It's just sucking the fun from every fan!

Why do comets always bring a snack?
They don't want to leave their tail out back!
When the universe calls, hold on tight,
It's got some cosmic jokes that may ignite!

Pulsar Punchlines

What did the asteroid say to its friend?
"You rock, but let's not pretend!"
Do you know why planets get along?
They always orbit just like a song!

Why was the sun always so bright?
Because it knew how to light up the night!
Neptune tried to tell a joke, so dry,
Mercury laughed, "Keep it cool, oh my!"

Starshine Snickers

A shooting star said, "Catch me if you can!"
But no one could, not even the man!
Black holes are like hidden jokes galore,
Funny how they always want more!

Why did the galaxy skip its class?
Because it thought it would never pass!
Stars gather round for a comedy night,
With laughter echoing into the light!

Cosmic Quips

Why do aliens never play cards?
They're afraid of the deck's hidden guards!
What's a meteor's favorite snack?
Anything that doesn't hold it back!

Why are planets so good at sports?
They know how to rotate in all sorts!
In the universe, laughter fuels flights,
Cosmic humor shines bright on starry nights!

Scintillating Satires

In the void, a bright wink,
Stars winking at black holes,
A cosmic game of hide-and-seek,
While asteroids steal the rolls.

Comets drop by for a chat,
Sweeping tails like a broom,
While aliens sip their tea,
In the vastness of the room.

Gravity's got a sly grin,
Pulling pranks on the moons,
Spinning them in dizzy loops,
Who knew they'd be so tunes?

Neutron stars host dance-offs,
Pulsing with a lively beat,
While planets shuffle awkwardly,
In shoes that just can't compete.

Cosmic Chronicles

A star once claimed to be wise,
But tripped on a meteor's tail,
Landed flat in a supernova,
Now stories tell the tale.

Galaxies argue and bicker,
Who has the shiniest bling?
While dark matter rolls its eyes,
At each glitzy fling.

Saturn's rings had a party,
The invite was lost in space,
Now all the moons are jealous,
Of its glamorous, grand embrace.

A black hole took up yoga,
Said it would find its zen,
Now it bends time and light,
But cannot fit in again.

Celestial Capers

In a nebula, folks chortle,
Stars throw a glittering bash,
While meteors moonwalk by,
In a bright, shimmering flash.

An alien lost his keys,
In a cluster of old dust,
Now he's stuck at the wormhole,
Dreaming of interstellar rust.

A stubborn sun tried to tan,
But ended up burnt to red,
Now it wears a halo bright,
And a wide-brimmed starry head.

Planets compete in a race,
But Jupiter hogs the lane,
While Mars just floats along,
Sipping on cosmic champagne.

Stellar Snaps

A light-year's just a small trip,
In a car with a rogue engine,
But that comet named Speedy,
Is the one always trendin'.

Nebulae keep taking selfies,
With filters from the abyss,
While black holes photobomb hard,
With a swirling dark kiss.

A rogue star told a tall tale,
That it danced with a quasar,
But the truth is still out there,
It's just a lonely memoir.

The Milky Way plays charades,
With dust bunnies and light rays,
While planets snicker softly,
At the dark matter's displays.

Outlandish Orbits

In the vastness of space, I took a wrong turn,
Zipping past planets, and feeling the burn.
A comet waved hi, I offered a snack,
'You're late for your orbit,' it gave me some flack.

Stars play cards, while the black holes yawn,
One bet a supernova, 'I'll see you at dawn!'
Galaxies dance, in a cosmic ballet,
But I tripped on a star, and now here I lay.

Celestial Chronicles

A space whale sings, in a pitch rare and high,
While Martians sip tea as the Earthcatch flies by.
Saturn's rings bling, 'We're the jewelry of space!'
But when they get dirty, it's a different chase.

Venus is smirking, it's hiding a wink,
While asteroids tumble, 'We're stars, don't you think?'
A rocket's hiccup led to a pie,
Flung through the ether, much to Mars' sly eye.

Cosmic Conundrums

Why did the asteroid cross the night sky?
To prove it was stardust and give dreams a try.
Neptune's got blue, but it's more than a hue,
It's the color of laughter from aliens too!

A moon tried to moonwalk, oh what a sight!
Fell flat on its face, in the soft cosmic night.
The sun wore shades, looking cool as can be,
But even it giggled, 'There's no tanning for me!'

Nebulae Nonsense

In nebulae thick, with colors galore,
A darling little quark asked, 'What's life in store?'
'Why float with the fluff, when you can dance all day?'
And so they twirled off, in a shimmering sway.

A black hole sneezed, and a galaxy spun,
Creating a whirlpool, oh what cosmic fun!
Stars wrapped in blankets, having a rave,
'What's the light show?' 'It's the tune that we crave!'

Celestial Chortles

In the sky there's a spark,
A star that dances in the dark.
Winks and giggles up above,
Who knew space could be so full of love?

Asteroids toss and turn with glee,
Shooting stars spill their tea.
Light-years make the best of pals,
Laughing out loud, even the quasar gals.

Black holes can't help but grin,
For every spin, there's a cosmic win.
They suck in jokes with all their might,
And shoot them back as comets of light.

Meteor showers blink and tease,
Creating chaos with the greatest ease.
They fall like laughter, swift and bright,
Making the galaxy a merry sight.

Physics of Fun

Gravity's got a sense of humor,
Pulling us down, like a fun rumor.
When you trip, don't take it hard,
The earth just wants to play its card.

Quantum leaps might seem quite bizarre,
Like jumping from here to a distant star.
But in the realm of the atomic jig,
Every little atom's got a dance gig.

Relativity lends a quirky twist,
Time ticks slower, who can resist?
In a time warp, you can stay a kid,
But where'd that hour go? Oh, it just hid!

Light travels fast, but jokes are quicker,
They shine so bright, they make us snicker.
In the cosmos of giggles, we all play nice,
In this universe, laughter's the best advice.

Starlit Satire

Stars align for a cosmic roast,
Each twinkling light, they're doing the most.
With puns so stellar, they're out of sight,
The Milky Way's giggling throughout the night.

Planets spin with a round of cheer,
While Saturn's rings hold a grand career.
Jupiter's got the biggest jokes in tow,
But he's just gassy; we already know.

Cosmic dust drifts on playful whims,
Creating laughter through seraphic hymns.
A nebula bursts, and with it, a jest,
As it colors the night, it's simply the best.

In the void where silence dwells,
Witty echoes of laughter swell.
Every supernova's a chance to play,
Truth be told, stars shine brighter that way.

Nova Narratives

Once upon a time, a star was born,
A brilliant flash that left us all worn.
"Did you see that?" the constellations say,
"Another great tale from light-years away!"

A comet zips with a cheeky grin,
As if it's racing to get back in.
With a tail of sparkles, it bows to the crowd,
Leaving behind a trail that's laughably loud.

Supernova parties? Oh, what a sight!
Exploding with joy, igniting the night.
With galactic streamers and cosmic cake,
Space is a funhouse, make no mistake!

In the heart of the cosmos, the cosmos hums,
A chorus of chuckles, oh how it drums!
For in this vastness where silliness reigns,
The stories of stars are the best of the gains.

Infinite Banter

In the depths of cosmic jest,
Stars giggle in their quest.
Planets dance with carefree grace,
While moons grin in their place.

Asteroids toss jokes like stones,
Rockets hum cheerful tones.
Galaxies spin tales so wide,
Nebulas chuckle, filled with pride.

Celestial beings share their glee,
Tickling comets, wild and free.
Each twinkle is a punchline bright,
Galactic humor, pure delight.

Cosmic Conundrums

Why did the star refuse to shine?
It lost its spark and wanted wine!
A black hole asked for more of light,
Said it's a party, outta sight!

Light years played hide and seek,
But dark matter said, "I'm too unique!"
Supernova's laughter burst so loud,
While comets formed a giggling crowd.

Stellar pranks are all the rage,
As planets flip to the cosmic stage.
Laughter echoed through the spheres,
Filling space with joyful cheers.

Astral Anecdotes

Once a star wore a silly hue,
To impress a lovely moon, it grew.
They sparkled in a waltzy dance,
While meteors tried to take a chance.

Mars cracked jokes while dressed in red,
"Why so serious?" the crowd then said.
Venus, with a wink and smile,
Brought laughter from a cosmic mile.

Planets shared their quirkiest tales,
As stardust giggled on flailing trails.
Saturn's rings sang a merry tune,
While asteroids played peek-a-boo, oh so soon!

Lightyear Laughs

In a race across the starry lanes,
Light beams laughed, ignoring pains.
A photon said with a cheeky flair,
"Catch me if you dare, I swear!"

Gravity's got its crushing jokes,
Sending asteroids in playful pokes.
Black holes snicker in shadows deep,
Enticing travelers to take a leap.

Wormholes twisted with a grin,
"Come on in, let the fun begin!"
Time traveled with a wink and nod,
Making space a stage quite odd.

Starlight Serenades

In the sky, stars play hide and seek,
A comet trips, oh what a peek!
Constellations giggle, twinkling bright,
Space has jokes, a dazzling sight.

When planets dance in a cosmic ball,
They twirl and stumble, won't catch a fall!
Shooting stars make wishes that gleam,
Even spacemen get lost in their dream.

Galaxies spin with a whirl and a twirl,
Dark matter's just shy; give it a whirl!
Asteroids wink, on asteroids ride,
In this universe, joy's amplified.

So next time you gaze at the night sky,
Don't just search for answers, laugh and fly!
For among the vastness, one truth stays clear,
The universe loves a good chuckle, my dear.

Nebula Narratives

In clouds of color, giggles bloom,
Stars whisper secrets while hiding their gloom.
A nova says, "Light show, step right up!"
While space-time keeps spilling cosmic cup.

Every black hole has a humor untold,
Swallowing light, but never too bold.
Supernovae throw parties, oh what a blast,
Dance like starlight, make your joy last!

From Mercury's mischief to Neptune's pranks,
Planets love jests, they send their thanks!
In the heart of the cosmos, smiles abound,
Space loves laughter, a joyous sound.

So let's toast to the night, to comets and beams,
To the humor of space and its whimsical dreams!
For in the universe, where laughter ignites,
A stitch in the stars makes everything bright.

Astral Banter

Lightyears away, hear the cosmic jest,
Planets trade jokes, it's truly the best!
Saturn laughs loudly, its rings in a spin,
While Mars holds its breath, hoping to win!

Jupiter's storms brew a laugh or two,
"Can you take this heat?" it jovially coos.
While asteroids chuckle in their rocky lane,
Space jokes are wild, and none are plain!

Aliens giggle in their ships from afar,
Trading their stories, a universal bazaar.
They say, "Why not travel? We'll share a snack!"
Cosmic picnics at noon, no gravity's lack.

So when you look up and the stars seem to grin,
Know there's more than just starlight within.
In the vastness of space, a smile takes flight,
Bantering boldly, through dark and through light.

Galactic Giggles

In the cosmic giggle, stars take a dip,
A nebula's twirl makes a colorful flip!
Planets have tickles, through all of their orbits,
Laughter erupts, no need for the sorbents!

Distant quasars play tag, faster than light,
While comets throw pies in the luminous night.
Even black holes pull pranks from their lair,
Spinning the tales of what's out there in the air!

Quirky galaxies swirl, a dance quite absurd,
Each flicker of light, a funny absurd word.
The Andromeda wink, the Milky Way grin,
Tells us sweet laughter resides deep within.

So join in the fun of this stellar ballet,
As the cosmos chuckles, joyfully plays.
For among the stars, in this mystical gig,
The universe whispers, "Dance, laugh, and dig!"

Quirk of the Cosmos

In the vastness, stars do wink,
Galaxies laugh, what do you think?
Black holes might lurk with a grin,
Sucking in light, where does it begin?

Whatever you do, don't take aim,
Space is silly, it's all a game.
Planets spin in their tidy suits,
Dancing 'round stars like cosmic brutes.

Meteor showers bring falling jokes,
While supernovae throw the best pokes.
Gravity pulls, but humor's free,
Floating in space is where we'll be.

Cosmic dust gathers with sly delight,
Creating new worlds in the night.
So laugh with the cosmos, take a shot,
In this universe, let's dance a lot!

Witty Universes

Check the stars for the punchline,
Jokes light-years deep, oh how they shine!
With big bangs of laughter in the void,
The universe plays, no need to avoid.

Nebulas bloom, like comics unfold,
With colors so rich, stories retold.
Asteroids crack jokes as they zip by,
Leaving trails that make us sigh.

Spaceships zoom with a honk and a cheer,
Alien jokes in the atmosphere near.
They giggle at light, run opaque marathons,
Warp-speed humor in stellar salons.

Gravity's grip may pull us apart,
But witty quips keep us close at heart.
In this crowded universe, let laughter play,
A cosmic carnival, join the fray!

Starstruck Smirks

Stars twinkle with cheeky delight,
Giggling as galaxies dance in the night.
Pluto's the one who can't take a hint,
Claiming he's "in", but others just squint.

Mars makes faces, all red and hot,
While Venus swoons with a plot twist not.
Comets go by with a tail full of sass,
Leaving us earthlings to laugh and pass.

Shooting stars giggle, wishes in tow,
"Make me a sandwich!" while traveling slow.
Constellations wink, clever shapes in the dome,
As humor shines bright, calling us home.

So clink your glasses, toast to the sky,
Every quirk in the cosmos, we'll never deny.
With smiles and chuckles, let's raise our cheer,
In a universe brimming with joy and cheer!

Comet's Comedy

Comets dash by with a plucky charm,
Spreading laughter, they mean no harm.
With tails of giggles that sweep and soar,
They promise a punchline and then some more!

In the cosmic theater where stars take stage,
The audience of planets reacts with rage.
"Too bright!" they shout, "tone it down!" they plead,
While laughter ignites like a cosmic seed.

Planets throw parties, rolling in glee,
With moonlit dances, all wild and free.
"Swing me around!" yells the Earth from the crowd,
As laughter erupts, vibrant and loud.

So look to the skies for the next great show,
Where humor abounds in the stardust glow.
Dance with space jokes and find your bliss,
In the grand comedy, give life a kiss!

Celestial Humor

A star walked into a bar, oh my,
The bartender said, 'You look high!'
The star replied with a twinkle bright,
'I'm just here to lighten the night!'

A comet sneezed, and to everyone's shock,
It sent little asteroids flying like a clock.
'Excuse me,' it said, 'I meant no harm,'
But the planets all laughed at its charm!

Neptune joked, 'I'm feeling quite blue,'
'Seems like my gas clouds need a view.'
Saturn chimed in, 'Join my ring, it's clear,'
'We can dance till the dawn, no fear!'

A black hole grinned, no need to pretend,
'I'm just here to pull you in, my friend!'
With a wink, it spun great tales of delight,
Leaving everyone chuckling into the night.

Interstellar Insights

Mars said, 'Eating dust all day,
Isn't the best, I must say!'
But with a giggle, it swung its red fist,
'At least I have moons to add to my list!'

The Milky Way stretched, feeling quite grand,
Said, 'I'm the best galaxy in the land!'
And while others rolled their stellar eyes,
It just smiled, 'Well, I'm full of surprise!'

A meteor shower was quite a sight,
With bits of laughter, dancing in flight.
'Catch us if you can, we're zooming fast!'
'These jokes are a blast, we're having a blast!'

Uranus joked, 'I am not what I seem,
With all of my rings, I'm quite the meme!'
Planets united, shared laughter galore,
In the cosmic play, who could ask for more?

Ethereal Jokes

A rogue planet strutted with flair,
'No orbits for me, I dance in midair!'
The sun chuckled bright, shining its rays,
'You'll miss your friends in so many ways!'

Pluto whispered, 'I'm still a tough little dude,'
'Tough love from the cosmos, but I've got the mood.'
With a laugh of its own, it waved a small flag,
'I'm the cutest; don't make me brag!'

Stars are just fiery balls of gas,
But don't bring them down; let them dance and sass.
They twinkle and giggle through the night sky,
'Just keep your wishes, we're never too shy!'

A wink from a satellite, circling in glee,
Said, 'I'll send you selfies, just for a fee!'
Planets erupted with joy in their play,
In the celestial fun, they laughed all day!

Gravity's Grin

Gravity chuckled, 'Don't float away!'
'To stay grounded is the best way.'
Planets rolled over, avoiding the pull,
'We'll stay close for the thrill, so cool!'

Asteroids tumbled in cosmic ballet,
'Watch out, folks, we'll steal your play!'
The stars flickered, sharing a joke,
'In space, nobody hears you poke!'

A neutron star boasted with pride,
'I've got density that won't subside!'
But with a wink and a playful tease,
'It's just a phase; I'll fit with ease!'

In the vastness, laughter echoed loud,
'We're a quirky bunch, we're eternally proud.'
Across the cosmos, the humor flows,
With every wink, each planet glows!

Galactic Fancies

In the sky where stars collide,
A comet slipped, but chose to glide.
It spun and twirled, what a sight!
"Hey, watch me dance!" it yelled in flight.

A planet bloomed a polka dot,
With rings of cheese, quite the plot!
Aliens cheered with cosmic flair,
"Let's host a picnic, oh, who's aware?"

Black holes laugh at the speed of light,
"Catch me if you can, hold on tight!"
They snicker deep in space's fold,
While shooting stars spin tales retold.

So if you gaze at the night so vast,
Remember the fun the universe cast.
With twinkling lights and silly scenes,
Space is wild with its zany dreams.

Nebula Nonsense

A blob of gas decided to play,
It painted the sky in a colorful way.
"Look at me swirl, I'm the star of the show!"
"Not bad for a cloud," said the moon with a glow.

A star named Sparky lost its bright shine,
"Can someone help? I tripped on a line!"
The universe chuckled, oh, what a sight,
As Sparky rolled over, again taking flight.

In a cosmic joke, planets collide,
"Oops, my bad!" both would chide.
With laughter echoing through the night,
They settled down with smiles so bright.

So let's embrace the cosmic cheer,
With nebula giggles that we hold dear.
Each twinkle and puff, a tale on cue,
In the wacky world of the sky so blue.

Radiant Riddles

Stars tell stories with sparkly grins,
But who cracks jokes when the laughter begins?
A space traveler leans in to say,
"Why did the stardust cross the Milky Way?"

To fly with a smile on a solar breeze,
And tease the black holes with cosmic tease!
"Is it dark in there?" asks the sun with a wink,
"Or just a swirling game of time in sync?"

A supernova popped like a party,
"This is my exit, it's going to be hearty!"
Galaxies chuckled and danced in delight,
"Onward, dear friend, to the great starlit night!"

With radiant riddles that spin and play,
The universe brightens each laugh-filled day.
So join in the jest, let your heart soar high,
For the cosmos has jokes that'll make you cry.

Stellar Chuckles

In a cosmic café where comets meet,
Stellar beings order laughs to eat.
A spike of starlight here and there,
"Hold the gravity!" they say with flair.

Jokes float past on solar winds,
As meteors chuckle and share their sins.
"Remember that time black holes took flight?
Their jokes were so heavy, they vanished from sight!"

Dwarfs danced round a helium fire,
"Who needs a menu? We'll never tire!"
Giggles and stars light up the scene,
Where laughter sparkles, and joy is keen.

So in the vastness, remember this,
The best of space is a stellar bliss.
With each funny tale, our hearts grow fonder,
In this universe, let laughter wander.

Dazzling Drollery

In the sky, a star wears a crown,
Winking at planets, never a frown.
Do comets grin when they swoosh past?
Or are they just trying to move fast?

A black hole joked, 'I'm full of mass!'
But everyone knows it just eats grass.
Galaxies giggle, swirling away,
While meteors rock out in their ballet.

Nebulas tangle in colorful threads,
Making costumes from dust, no less said.
Cosmic laughter, a delightful sound,
Echoes through space, so profound.

So let's toast the stars with a cheer,
For the cosmic comedy we hold dear.
With every twinkle and radiant flare,
The universe is laughing—be aware!

Space Laughs

Gravity's pull can be such a tease,
Bouncing like crazy, knees to the breeze.
Planets spin round like they're at a fair,
Dizzy from axis, but they don't care!

Asteroids crack jokes as they collide,
'This rock's too big, better run and hide!'
While satellites dance to a satellite song,
Orbiting rhythms, they just can't go wrong.

Stars play peekaboo, hiding from view,
'Catch me if you can!' is their giggle too.
Aliens chuckle in their little ships,
Laughing at Earthling's odd little quips.

In this cosmic circus, what a sight,
Where every twist brings joy and delight.
So, lift your spirits and gaze above—
The universe's humor is full of love!

Comet Caped Capriccios

A comet's tail is a fashion spree,
Streaming bright, as if to say, 'Look at me!'
In a cosmic cape, it dodges and weaves,
Twirling through stars like autumn leaves.

Meteorites crash with a sparkly cheer,
Saying, 'Let's party, we've all made it here!'
While distant worlds hide their giggles inside,
As comet parades in a glittering glide.

Planets throw confetti of stardust and glee,
As supernovas light up the spree.
There's joy in the void, humor in glare,
With each cosmic wink, there's laughter to share.

So if you glance up, give a good wink,
Join in the fun, let your thoughts sink.
The universe dances, a joyous ballet,
In the grandest show, come what may!

Dark Matter Dramas

In shadows where mysteries often dance,
Dark matter chuckles at secrets askance.
Invisible friends in a cosmic game,
Playing hide and seek, but never the same.

Black holes throw parties, but lose track of time,
Inviting all stardust with pizzazz and mime.
They say, 'Don't get close, it's a wild ride!'
Yet everyone giggles, enjoying the tide.

Pulsars pulse to a tick-tock tune,
Making time guests move to the moon.
They say, 'Can't stop, we're just blinking, you see!'
In the laughter of space, set your spirit free.

The cosmos is playful, a whimsical scene,
Where both light and dark know what fun can mean.
Embrace every mystery wrapped in delight,
For the universe laughs in the still of the night!

Starlit Smirks

In the vastness above, a comet did zoom,
Its tail just a wink, like a playful broom.
Stars giggle and wink, a celestial jest,
A dance of delight that's simply the best.

Planets swirl round in their orbits of glee,
One tripped on its ring, oh what sight to see!
Saturn laughed loud, with its rings all aglow,
While Jupiter chuckled, 'That's one way to show!'

A meteor shower, a sparkly show,
Some fell with a splat, much to their woe.
'Next time try landing, not flying in haste,'
Said Venus with laughter, all glitter and paste.

So when gazing up at the magnificent night,
Remember the laughter that fills the starlight.
For in space, even orbs have their fun,
With starlit smirks shared by everyone.

Astronomical Antics

A star once declared it would start a band,
With aliens dancing in a cosmic strand.
They practiced for eons, but couldn't agree,
On whether to jam with a sax or a bee.

The black hole DJ spins records so tight,
While quasars beam tunes in the velvet night.
Asteroids clapped, but forgot how to sway,
Stuck in a rock, they'd just roll away.

Galaxies twirled, each one with a name,
But when it came to rhythms, it's all the same.
They boogied and bounced in a spiral of fun,
Only to trip and collapse, one by one.

Remember the stars when you laugh at the night,
Their antics and giggles are pure delight.
For in this vast cosmos, plays out a show,
Of astronomical sillies, like none that you know.

Melodies of the Milky Way

A rocket took flight on a whimsical scheme,
With a playlist of tunes and a sweet ice cream.
The satellites hummed, trying to sing along,
But the harmony slipped and turned into a gong.

Meteorites danced on the beat they made,
While stars popped confetti in a bright cascade.
The planets, all laughing, rolled with delight,
As the galaxy giggled through the whimsical night.

A cosmic DJ with a twist in his hat,
Dropped a funky beat that made everyone bat.
Comets shot by with a glittering grin,
Scribbling the notes with a brilliant spin.

So join in the fun of this stellar ballet,
With melodies floating in the Milky Way.
For every bright note brings joy to your day,
In the cosmic concert where we all want to play.

Universal Uproar

In the depths of space, a ruckus was heard,
As Venus and Mars joined a wobbly herd.
They stomped on the comets, twirled round the moons,
Creating a ruckus that echoed like tunes.

A galaxy-wide race had just taken flight,
Stars zoomed by laughing, it felt just right.
But one little asteroid forgot how to steer,
Slammed into a nebula, igniting good cheer.

The sun cracked a joke, but it got lost in rays,
As planets burst out with their hilarious ways.
Every black hole let out a giggly shout,
"Come join the uproar, let's dance all about!"

So if you're feeling low, just look to the sky,
For the universe beams where the stars like to fly.
In every new twinkle, a joyous encore,
Echoes in laughter, this universal uproar.

Nova's Nonsense

In the cosmos, stars like to bicker,
One twinkled bright, the other flicker.
They argued who shone a tad more bright,
Until the moon chimed in, 'It's late tonight!'

Galaxies swirl in a dizzy dance,
Comets zoom by with a comedic prance.
A black hole yawned, what a big scare,
Sucking in jokes with an endless flair.

A satellite laughed, it lost its way,
'Thanks to gravity, I'm a must-see stray!'
Shooting stars made a wish, oh so rare,
But tripped on stardust—what a blare!

Planets chuckled in their merry spins,
Mercury teased, 'I've got the quick wins!'
While Venus blushed in her shimmery gown,
Said, 'Why so serious, let's clown around!'

Astronomical Laughter

In the realm of stars, tales are spun,
Jupiter joked, 'I'm the big, round one!'
Saturn chimed in with rings so bright,
'At least I can wear them; what a delight!'

A meteor shower began to jest,
Made a splash and tried to impress.
Laser beams shot with a zing and a zap,
They whizzed around like a cosmic rap.

Uranus smirked with a galaxy grin,
'Wanna hear a joke? Where do I begin?'
While little Pluto, out in the cold,
Said, 'Even I'm funny, if truth be told!'

The stardust fairies floated in glee,
'Tell a joke about space? Yes! Count me!'
The cosmos roared with laughter so loud,
Even the comets gathered a crowd!

Lighthearted Orbits

Orbits are funny, a looping game,
Earth told the moon, 'You're rather lame!'
But the moon winked back, 'I have a glow,
You're still just a rock; let's get this show!'

Asteroids giggled, bumping in flight,
'We just wanna dance through the starry night!'
They jived and they jiggled, fell into space,
Twirling around like they won a race.

The sun, full of warmth, loves to play,
Said, 'I'm the brightest; who's here to stay?'
Stars nodded in rhythm, a dazzling sight,
'Join the troupe, let's glow through the night!'

In this universe, laughter ignites,
With planets and moons sharing funny sights.
They spin and they twirl on their endless course,
In a dance of delight, a comedic force!

Universe of Whimsy

In the cosmic sea, where sillies abide,
Celestial bodies take laughter for a ride.
A neutron star grinned with neutron delight,
Said, 'I'm dense but my jokes are light!'

Astro-animals peek with bright eyes,
A dog with a comet, oh what a surprise!
They frolic through space, tails wagging along,
Chasing constellations, singing their song.

Time-traveling clocks tick-tock in cheer,
Confusing the stars, 'Wait, when are we here?'
Galactic giggles ripple through the void,
As laughter reveals what the cosmos enjoyed.

So gather your stardust, bring forth a grin,
In this whimsical universe, let the fun begin.
With echoes of humor from far and near,
The cosmos invites us, 'Come join us here!'

Intergalactic Jests

In a galaxy far, laughter takes flight,
Alien comedians shine so bright.
With jokes made of stardust, talent galore,
They tickle your funny bone and leave you wanting more.

Space puns take off, like rockets on cue,
'Why did the moon break up? Too much space, it's true!'
Planets spin round, they dance to the tune,
Cracking up Saturn, who just lost his ring to the moon.

A comet once tripped on an asteroid's tail,
'Gravity's a hoot!' it shouted, turning pale.
Black holes chuckle, spitting light like confetti,
In the vast cosmos, the laughter's never petty.

So join the starlit jests, don't miss the beam,
In the universe of humor, it's all a dream!
Fresh cosmic quips, a galactic delight,
We float in giggles, through the endless night.

Solar Silliness

The sun winks down with a radiant grin,
'Why don't I ever play cards? I can't deal with the spin!'
The planets giggle, as they twirl in their dance,
While comets slip by, taking silly chance.

Mercury's quick, with a zippy little joke,
'Sometimes I feel heated, but never go broke!'
Venus blushes bright, with a light-hearted twist,
'I'm not just a planet, I also insist!'

Jupiter's laughs echo from the great storm,
'Thought I was flat? Just keeping my form!'
While Saturn's rings gleam with a shimmer so bright,
'I just got new bling; I'm ready for a night!'

So gather the rays and the giggles of light,
In this sunny jest fest, everything's bright!
Solar silliness shines, as the days drift away,
In a cosmos delight, where laughter can play.

Void Verses

In the deep, dark void, whispers are heard,
A black hole chuckles, not saying a word.
'Why did the star break up? Too much space in between!'
The galaxies giggle at this cosmic scene.

Nebulae swirl with colors so bold,
'This cloud's got jokes—let them unfold!'
'A neutron walks into a bar, what a fright!
The bartender shouts, 'You're negative tonight!'

An empty expanse where the silence can scream,
Yet laughter erupts like a bubbling stream.
Comets zoom by with a wink and a jest,
'Longer than light, we're on a fun quest!'

So float through the void, where the punchlines collide,
In the universe's laughter, there's nowhere to hide.
With each quirky twist, in the vastness we play,
Even in emptiness, we find joy on display.

Phases of Humor

The moon shifts shapes, from full to a sliver,
Cracking jokes, making all the stars quiver.
'Today I'm a crescent, so playful and spry,
I tell shadows to laugh as the night passes by.'

The sun bursts out, a giant ball of cheer,
'What did one photon say? "Let's make this clear!"'
As night falls softly, with a wink and a nod,
Lunar giggles arise from the cosmic facade.

'Tripping over starlight, one comet exclaimed,
Why commute to Earth? When the sky's already famed!'
Each planet takes turns, sharing stories of glee,
The universe spins on, happy and free.

So embrace every phase, let the laughter unfold,
In the cosmic phases, humor's pure gold!
Through shadows and light, let the giggles persist,
In the playground of stars, we can't resist!

Galactic Gags

In the starry sky, a clown does soar,
Painting planets with laughter that we adore.
Each comet's tail, a banana peel,
Slipping through space, what a cosmic wheel!

Aliens giggle in their greenish suits,
Chasing space cows in starry boots.
They tickle a moon with a feather light,
Turning the orbits into a silly sight.

Nebulae whisper jokes that are grand,
While asteroids dance, forming a band.
A pulsar blinks, playfully it winks,
As galaxies chuckle amidst the brinks.

In the void, a quip takes flight,
Astro-bunnies hop with delight.
With every star, a punchline gleams,
In the universe of humor, nothing's as it seems.

Black Hole Buffoonery

Down by the black hole, it's quite the show,
Where time bends funny, and nobody knows.
With spacetime stretched, and humor unfurled,
It's a gravity well of the wacky world.

A star gets sucked in, wearing a hat,
Says, "What a ride! Can you believe that?"
A cosmic joker with a twinkle in sight,
Pulling in giggles as it swallows the night.

Singularity spins, doing the twist,
While the universe laughs, unable to resist.
Planets collide, sharing their puns,
In the comedy club where the light never runs.

So if you're lost in that swirling delight,
Just remember to chuckle, it'll be alright.
For even in darkness, the laughter won't cease,
In the depths of the cosmos, find your inner peace.

Celestial Whispers

Stars whisper secrets in cosmic tones,
Joking about comets and their rolling stones.
"Why don't they ever land?" one star jokes with glee,
"Because their schedules are too spaced-out, you see!"

Moons giggle softly in orbiting loops,
As meteors slide down in goofy swoops.
One says, "Watch out, it's a starry rain!"
"Catch one! They are brilliant—but hard to maintain!"

Clustered configurations in a starry choir,
Harmony found in a galactic fire.
Their chants echo forth, a melody bright,
Bursting with laughter, lighting up the night.

In this cosmic dance, where shadows blend,
Watch for the punchlines that twist and bend.
Celestial whispers weave tales full of cheer,
In the fabric of space, the humor is clear.

Cosmic Jests

In the nebula's joke shop, fun floats around,
Stars swap their knock-knock jokes, laughing unbound.
"Knock, knock!" says Mars, "Who's there in the night?"
"Luna! Just lunar, don't put out your light!"

Asteroids tumble like barrels of laughs,
While Saturn spins tales about its cool gaffes.
"What did the rings say to the lonely star?"
"Join the party, we'll go really far!"

Meteor showers pelt with playful delight,
While cosmic creatures frolic under the light.
Each burst of laughter brightens the dark,
As galaxies groove, creating a spark.

So float on through space with a grin on your face,
And revel in humor, find your own place.
In the universe's jest, joy meets the quest,
Creating a cosmos where laughter is best.

Nebulous Wit

In the clouds of space, a joke would stray,
Starships laughing, in their own way.
Lightyears pass, but who has the time?
Falling asteroids hum a silly rhyme.

A comet tripped on its icy tail,
Told the Sun, "I'm bound to fail!"
But giggles echoed through the void,
As planets swirled and stars enjoyed.

Cosmic dancers in a wobbly spin,
Slipped on gravity, forgot to grin.
Alien beings with a punchline quite bold,
Said, "Your universe is getting old!"

Through the Milky Way, the humor rolled,
With every supernova, a new tale told.
In the heart of darkness, laughter ignites,
As even black holes keep the jokes light.

Twilight Tales

At dusk when stars begin to play,
Meteors dance in a comical sway.
A funny asteroid tried to park,
But hit a nebula, made it dark!

On Saturn's rings, a race was set,
Flying fast, they made a bet.
Rings got tangled like a joke gone wrong,
While Moons chimed in with a silly song.

Galactic giggles filled the air,
As stardust swirled everywhere.
Jupiter sighed with a jovial grin,
"Why did the star avoid a spin?"

"Because it didn't want to lose its glow!"
Echoed laughter, the tales would flow.
In this vast twilight, mirth takes flight,
And space is bright with pure delight.

Astronomical Amusements

In the cosmic circus, stars take their turn,
Planets juggle, as comets learn.
A supernova dropped its big act,
And caused a ripple in space-time pact.

Meanwhile, black holes became the jesters,
Sucking in jokes from cosmic testers.
"Catch me if you can!" they slyly called,
But gravity giggled, they both just stalled.

A spacecraft zoomed by with a horn,
Said, "I'm too cool for this cosmic yarn!"
But on its way, it hit a star,
Bouncing back, it exclaimed, "Not too far!"

At the edge of the universe, laughter reigns,
Twirling in time with its funny gains.
Every twinkle holds a story to tell,
In the grand amusement park of the celestial swell.

Orbital Oddities

In orbit, they spun, the strangest sights,
Comets with wigs and meteors in tights.
A Saturnian told a pun to the Moon,
"Why was the nebula late? It lost its tune!"

Galaxies twirled in a quirky dance,
Supernovae laughed, as if by chance.
"Why did the star bring a ladder today?
To reach for a joke in the Milky Way!"

In this bizarre cosmos, laughter entwined,
With planets grinning, their fates aligned.
Aliens giggled, with wide-open eyes,
As laughter echoed beneath the skies.

So when you gaze at the night's dark sea,
Remember, the universe loves a spree.
With each little twinkle, a giggle shines bright,
In this realm of oddities, pure delight!

Light-Year Laughs

In the vastness of space, what do stars do?
They twinkle and snicker, just like me and you!
When black holes play hide and seek with glee,
They're just trying to grab the light, can't you see?

A comet zooms past with a tail so bright,
"Hey Jupiter, look! I can fly in the night!"
But while it goes speeding, it trips on a moon,
And laughs echo out, like a cosmic cartoon.

Asteroids rolling, they think they're so tough,
Bumping each other, pretending they're rough.
But once they collide, oh what a surprise,
They giggle and scatter, no need for goodbyes!

A satellite chuckles, "I'm all alone!"
Yet hears the planets gossiping, moan.
In this cosmic circus, delight is the key,
We're all just space clowns, floating endlessly.

Constellation Capers

In the sky's tapestry, stars play a game,
Who can form the silliest picture, not fame?
Orion's just posing like a model so fine,
While the Pleiades giggles, "Look, we're a line!"

A fox in the sky tries to catch up a hare,
But all that they do is float round in air.
With a wink and a nudge, they wave to the sun,
"We're hunting for laughter; come join us for fun!"

Ursa Major grumbles, "My stars are too bright!"
While the Little Bear throws a cosmic delight.
They dance in their orbits, under moonlit beams,
A galactic ballet, where humor redeems.

Stars trade their jokes like candy at fairs,
While planets nod softly, with twinkling glares.
In this cosmic caper, we all play our part,
With laughter and joy, let's brighten the heart.

Radiant Riddles

What do you call an astronaut's favorite song?
Something that's stellar and can't be wrong!
Why did Mars break up with Saturn, you see?
Too many rings, it was too clingy!

In the universe wide, a riddle found light,
Why can't aliens play cards at night?
Because they're afraid of the deck getting shifty,
And the ghosts of the stars make their humor quite nifty!

An eclipse cheekily whispers, "I'm partly shy!"
While the sun simmers down, casting rays in reply.
"What's black and white, and never is seen?
A zebra in space, on a cosmic screen!"

Cosmic clowns frolic, turning stardust to laughs,
While Saturn's rings take their old photographs.
In the dance of the skies, the bright jokes entwine,
With radiant riddles, we feel so divine!

Interstellar Ironies

In a black hole's embrace, life's a twist,
You might ponder, "Where is it I missed?"
But space-time giggles, it's tricky and sly,
It's the ultimate trap—to never say bye!

What irony dwells in a star's bright song?
It sings light-years away, "I've been gone too long!"
While aliens ponder on selfies and fame,
Their signal gets lost on a cosmic game!

The neutron star, so dense, ponders fate,
"Why so serious? Life should be great!"
It spins with abandon, a disco delight,
While dark matter dances, hidden from sight.

Planets collide and create quite a fuss,
"Oops, I didn't see you! My space ship is rust!"
In the galaxy's whimsy, where all things align,
Interstellar ironies make our stars shine!

Celestial Jests

In the cosmos, stars do play,
They sprinkle laughs in a cheeky way.
A comet swings with silly flair,
While planets giggle in cosmic air.

Moons tease suns with a cosmic grin,
While black holes chuckle, pulling us in.
A meteor stumbles, then takes a bow,
Leaving stardust laughter here and now.

Galaxies collide with a wink and jest,
Creating chaos, oh what a fest!
We dance through space with silly tunes,
Tickled by rays from mischief's balloons.

So let's toast to the humor of night,
As stars share jokes, oh what a sight!
In this vast universe, let laughter roam,
Find joy in the cosmos, our celestial home.

Starlit Whispers

Hear the stars whisper cheesy lines,
They chuckle softly, like aged wines.
Planets spin with a giggly twist,
Their laughter echoing, none can resist.

Nebulas dance in vibrant hues,
Sharing secrets and cosmic clues.
A star went shopping but bought a sun,
Now it's glowing, oh what fun!

Saturn's rings jingle, a merry sound,
As moons play tag, spinning around.
Asteroids wobble, making faces,
In the vast void, joy embraces.

So join the night with a playful heart,
With starlit whispers, let laughter start.
For even in darkness, there's light to find,
In the cosmic giggles, let us unwind.

Cosmic Giggles

Twirling comets with wigs so bright,
Leave stardust trails, what a sight!
Neptune chuckles at his own blue,
While Mars plays dress-up, oh who knew?

The Milky Way holds a comedy show,
Where giants joke, and dwarfs steal the glow.
Eclipses happen with a wink at best,
As laughter rounds up the solar zest.

Black holes blurt, 'We're just sucking in!'
While stars reply, 'We're here to spin!'
Galactic giggles burst like balloons,
In the tapestry of celestial tunes.

So float through the cosmos, enjoy the ride,
With cosmic giggles, let joy abide.
For in every star's winking gleam,
Lies a little laughter, a cosmic dream.

Luminous Laughter

Underneath sky so vast and wide,
Stars beam down with a cheeky pride.
They shine bright with a playful grin,
While meteors race, ready to win.

Jupiter rolls with its jovial dance,
Encouraging moons to join in the prance.
A solar flare bursts with a snicker,
Leaving us laughing, our hearts grew thicker.

Each shooting star brings a joke to tell,
While space dust giggles, casting a spell.
The night sky sparkles with luminous cheer,
As galaxies gather for laughter to hear.

So let's journey on, 'neath the starlit skies,
With luminous laughter, let giggles arise.
In the space between planets, joy can be found,
In the play of the heavens, we all spin around.

Celestial Chuckles

In space there's a star that plays games,
It tickles the cosmos and draws funny names.
With each twinkle and flash,
It dances in a crash,
And leaves us all giggling like we're all the same.

But what does it wear for a celestial dress?
A cloak made of stardust, no need to impress.
It twirls with such flair,
In the weightless air,
While comets just chuckle, they couldn't care less.

There's a black hole that whispers a joke,
It swallows the punch line—oh, what a poke!
The universe roars,
As it opens new doors,
And the planets all laugh till they finally choke.

A sunbeam with mischief, oh what a sight,
Plays pranks on the moons, causing giggles so bright.
It hides behind clouds,
Then pops out and loud,
Shining laughter across the soft, starry night.

Luminous Limericks

A comet once danced on a whim,
With a tail that looked shockingly dim.
It slipped on a cloud,
And giggled aloud,
Saying, 'Next time, I'll aim for the rim!'

There once was a star with a smile,
Whose brightness could stretch for a mile.
It winked at a moon,
And sang quite a tune,
While the asteroids joined in with style.

A planet with stripes loved to tease,
It wore silly hats just to please.
When children looked up,
They laughed 'til they'd sup,
Saying, 'Gravity's just a disease!'

A satellite tried out a hat,
But it landed atop a fat cat.
The giggling poor sphere,
Thought it might steer,
Then fell with a thud—how about that!

Heavenly Humor

A star fell in love with a moon,
But their dance was a clumsy cartoon.
They tripped on the light,
Caused a comical fright,
And laughed through the night with a swoon.

In the hills of bright meteors rare,
A rocket made friends with a chair.
It zoomed with delight,
In a wild, wacky flight,
While the aliens giggled, quite fair.

A nebula painted in hues,
Told jokes with the funniest views.
It whispered to space,
With a smile on its face,
Leaving all of the black holes confused.

An asteroid couldn't find its way,
It danced in a most wobbly sway.
With each little bop,
It could hardly stop,
Saying, 'I'll reach home someday!'

Orbit of Oddities

There's a planet that loves to play tag,
With asteroids, it's never a drag.
Around and around,
They bound and rebound,
In a loop that's as odd as a brag.

A star tried to play peek-a-boo,
But its brightness just shined right on through.
The comets all laughed,
At the unplanned draft,
As they zipped past with glee, it's true.

An alien pet wore a shoe,
Said, 'This style's the latest, who knew?'
With a sparkle and grin,
It twirled round and in,
Leaving stardust and mischief to strew.

A solar flare made quite the scene,
Riding waves like a wild, wacky dream.
It danced with delight,
In the soft, starry night,
As the galaxies giggled in gleam.

Celestial Comedies

In the sky, the stars do jest,
They wear their crowns with silly zest.
A shooting star slipped on a beam,
And tumbled down, just like a dream.

Black holes giggle, twisting time,
While planets dance in perfect rhyme.
Mars boasts that he's the hottest host,
But Venus grins, a fiery ghost.

Uranus laughs at its own name,
Each joke rehearsed, yet all the same.
The sun shines bright, a radiant clown,
With solar flares that twirl around.

So in the night, let laughter rise,
As cosmic humor fills the skies.
In this vast space, with a wink and leap,
The universe holds secrets deep.

Interstellar Idiosyncrasies

A comet with a quirky tail,
Swore it would always leave a trail.
But in a twirl, it lost control,
And became a cosmic ginger roll.

Saturn spins with rings that sing,
While Jupiter boasts of its giant bling.
But secretly, all the moons agree,
Earth tells the best jokes on a spree.

Mars once tried to cook a stew,
But every ingredient just flew.
"Not a chef!" it cried in fright,
As meteors crashed left and right.

So gather 'round the galaxy wide,
Where the planets laugh, they do not hide.
With idiosyncrasies bright as stars,
The universe is one big joke bazaar.

Planetary Pranks

Earth wrapped the moon in tinsel fine,
While laughing at the stars that shine.
A prankster planet gave a spin,
As Martians danced, the games begin.

Neptune made a bubble bath,
And splashed around with giddy laugh.
But Pluto shouted, "I'm still here!"
Still waiting for a party cheer.

Venus dressed up in foam and fluff,
Claiming beauty's tough, but not enough.
The asteroids took sides to cheer,
For every silly prank they'd steer.

In space's vast and funny play,
The orbits twist in their own way.
With laughter echoing near and far,
The cosmos glows, a silly bazaar.

Spacetime Satirical Scenes

Time bends in ways that tickle fancy,
A wormhole leads to a cosmic dance spree.
Galaxies whisper in jokes so sly,
As gravity pulls us all awry.

Stars swap tales of many a quirk,
While cosmic dust's the perfect perk.
A black hole chuckles, eating light,
Saying, "Meals here are quite the sight!"

The sun throws shade with playful flare,
While comets race in joyous dare.
"Catch me if you can!" they tease and glide,
A spiral of laughter in cosmic tide.

So float along this funny ride,
Where space and time are giggly wide.
In the vastness of stars so bright,
A satirical scene ignites the night.

Supernova Smiles

In the cosmos, stars do play,
Twinkling jokes from far away.
A comet's tail, a wink so bright,
Shooting stars, a giggle in flight.

Galaxies spin in a dizzy dance,
Pulsars prance, oh take a chance!
A black hole's joke, it pulls you in,
Where all the laughter's lost in sin.

Planets roll in a cosmic spree,
Mars cracks jokes, as cheeky as can be.
Asteroids chuckle, in a rocky way,
Throwing humor like space confetti play.

Distant moons wink in playful tease,
While meteors rush like they're late for cheese.
In this vast sky, don't take it so serious,
Laughter's the fuel, oh so curious!

Luminary Laugh Lines

Stars shine bright, with humor to share,
Witty remarks float through the air.
A solar flare with comedic flair,
Lighting up space with a cosmic dare.

Galactic giggles swirl around,
In the void, funny echoes abound.
Nebulae chuckle, in colors so bold,
Painting laughter, stories untold.

Superstars crack a joke or two,
While orbiting bodies join the crew.
Astro-nuts laugh, they've got no shame,
Spinning tales, it's all just a game.

Infinity's full of jokes and cries,
Comedic wonders that light up the skies.
With every nova, laughter ignites,
In this universe, pure joy invites!

Universe Unplugged

In the dark, a stellar joke blooms,
Galaxies giggle in velvet rooms.
Dark matter hums a tune so sly,
Singing punchlines that float on by.

A space-time riddle unfolds with glee,
Wormholes twist, oh can't you see?
Gravity's pull can't hold back fun,
As cosmic clowns on their circus run.

Asteroids tumble with quips galore,
As rockets punch in, "Did we land before?"
They say, "There's no planet like home,"
Yet here we laugh, through the cosmic foam.

Nebulas blush in colors so bright,
As stardust sprinkles the cosmic light.
The universe laughs, a delight to behold,
In the humor of voids, true stories are told!

Stellar Satire

In the void, a pun takes flight,
Neutron stars say, "Oh that's light!"
Jovian jests from the gas giants sway,
While comets laugh in the Milky Way.

Pluto moans, "Where's my planet pass?"
Next to Neptune, he's made to sass.
Black holes whisper with a sly grin,
"Come a little closer, let's suck you in!"

Meteor showers rain down wit,
Falling from space in a humor fit.
Astro-onomers giggle at each blip,
As the cosmos prepares for a laughter trip.

Stars twinkle down with a wink of surprise,
"Did we just talk? Or were those the skies?"
And the universe chuckles, a laughter so grand,
In this cosmic show, it's all well planned!

Celestial Cabaret

Twinkling stars do dance and sway,
In the sky's vast cabaret play.
A comet slips on cosmic ice,
Laughing as it twirls—oh, how nice!

Planets juggling moons with glee,
One drops a ring, 'Oh, look at me!'
Asteroids in funny hats parade,
While Saturn's friends all serenade.

Galaxies gossip on a whim,
Shooting stars make wishes grim.
The universe, a grand delight,
With all its quirks, it shines so bright!

And as the comets zoom and scoot,
Cosmic clowns play games astute.
They flip and tumble through the vast,
In this cabaret, joy holds fast.

Luminous Laugh Wits

In the dark, light beams a grin,
As the solar breeze begins to spin.
Planets whisper jokes to the sun,
'Why did the moon bring a gun?'

Twinkling wit in cosmic flight,
Stars insist they shine so bright.
A starlit sage with funny lines,
Cracks up the cosmos with punchy signs.

Nebulae chuckle, colors collide,
Asteroid bands, no need to hide.
The Milky Way's a comedy show,
Where laughter rolls and chuckles grow.

Shooting stars share tales of woe,
Only to dance and steal the show.
With luminous laugh wits in full bloom,
The universe becomes an endless room.

Comedic Cosmos

The cosmos sings a comedic tune,
With stars that twinkle and silvery moon.
Galaxies spin, each one a skit,
While black holes try to catch a bit!

Space-time giggles with every leap,
As quasars play hide and seek with deep.
The sun cracks jokes about its rays,
Brightening up all lazy days.

Asteroids toss silly jabs and jests,
Making meteors laugh like guests.
The comical cosmos, a riotous place,
Where laughter sparkles through time and space.

Cosmic humor, a bolt of glee,
In this vastness, we're all carefree.
The universe chuckles, it's simply a must,
In this comedic realm, we place our trust.

Comedic Celestials

Comedic celestials gather round,
With cosmic laughter, a joyous sound.
Venus claims she's the fairest of all,
While Mars cracks jokes, having a ball.

Venus slips, and with style she lands,
Holding her pearls with shaky hands.
'Uranus tells tales of farts in space,
And all the orbs laugh in one embrace.

Jupiter's storms turn into a show,
With thunderous laughter all aglow.
While Saturn spins rings in a dance,
Creating a spectacle, a cosmic chance.

These celestial jesters in the night,
Paint the heavens with jokes that delight.
Life's a stage in this stellar scene,
Where every comet involves a routine!

www.ingramcontent.com/pod-product-compliance
Ingram Content Group UK Ltd.
Pitfield, Milton Keynes, MK11 3LW, UK
UKHW021359290125
4349UKWH00005B/38